How to Keep the Bill Collectors Off, Eat, and Keep a Roof Over Your Head If You Lose Your Job

Nicol

For more information:
Lady Intelligence, Ltd.
www.ladyintelligence.com

ISBN-13: 978-1493717330
ISBN-10: 1493717332

Published 2013
CreateSpace - Printed in the United States of America

This book is available at special quantity discounts for bulk purchases for sales promotions, premiums, fund-raising, or educational use. Special books, or book excerpts, can also be created to fit specific needs.

For details write:
Lady Intelligence, Ltd.
PO Box 24815
Lyndhurst, OH 44124
Attn: Special Markets
Or visit: www.ladyintelligence.com

~ Everything is going to be all right. ~

TABLE OF CONTENTS

INTRODUCTION

If you are reading this book, it is because of one of four things:

1. You have been given an idea that your job will no longer be available in the future,
2. You are currently in between jobs,
3. Somebody who cares about you and your situation gave this book to you, or
4. You're curious and want to be as informed as possible about anything and everything.

If you are reading this book, you may have also structured your life around pay periods and paychecks. Some of you may be one check or a half a check away from financial devastation and the last thing you need is for just on one payday, there will be no paycheck.

You may be single, married, have young loved ones, or have elderly loved ones - all of whom depending on that same paycheck. You may have been on the job for 10 months thinking that things would be okay. You might have been on the job for 15 to 20 years with slash marks on the calendar counting the couple of weeks, months, or years to retirement.

Not too long ago, if we knew of anybody who had a government job, we believed that the government worker would be set for life as long as they stayed on that job. Today, we are certain there is no such thing as job security. Not even for a federal worker.

We also thought that unemployment, social security, and welfare resources such as cash, food, and medical assistance were the safety nets that would always be in place in unforeseen circumstances. Today, we know that there are no guaranteed safety nets if there were to be any external safety nets at all.

There is nothing scarier about job elimination when the entire household's stability is dependent on that job. Even worse is trying to figure out what to do next and making sure that, for the most part, all steps are taken to replace the check that had been the lifeline to keep things afloat.

"How To Keep The Bill Collectors Off, Eat, and Keep a Roof Over Your Head If You Lose Your Job" will assist the income or wage earner that has never been forced to involuntarily say goodbye to a job and who is forced to figure out how to pay the bills and expenses that will continue to come. Information in this book will be helpful in making those initial steps to help maintain some sort of continuity in the household and for the family.

The Purpose of this Book/Disclaimer From the Author

The purpose of this book is to give you a guideline on what you need to do in suggested order and what to watch out for to keep the continuity of your current lifestyle as much as possible. Everything in this book is based upon my own personal and specific experiences and the research involved was the research necessary and specific for me to maintain my household.

Although, I have experience in consumer financial counseling, this book is only to convey information based upon my personal experience.

As you go through this book, you must contact your county and state regarding specific guidelines as it comes to applying and receiving unemployment compensation and welfare benefits, as well as for guidelines for any other social services or programs as each county within a state does things differently as well as each state within the United States of America.

Important Note: I am not an attorney. Again, anything written in this book is based upon my personal experience and my own personal interpretation of any processes or procedures. Consult an attorney within your city, county, or state for advice regarding your legal rights and any specific laws including all current policies and procedures.

About Your Bills

The important things that you need to do and have your mind on are eating and keeping a roof over your head. The bill collectors will call you until you break down and make a payment arrangement that will be difficult to keep as the weeks go by.

You can't give anything you don't have. Yes, they can seize your bank accounts and put a lien on your property, but there is a process to do so - so there is no need to panic. More will be covered on this in the "The Bill Collectors" chapter.

In the meantime, answer their phone call once and tell them your situation. Follow up that conversation with a letter. Save any letters that they may have sent to you. Do not make any arrangements with them until you've read "The Bill Collectors" and other bill collection and debt related segments in this book.

FIRST THINGS FIRST

There is nothing more important in this book than this segment. These steps are the absolute first steps you must take before doing anything else.

Get Your Mind In Order

You may be experiencing a sense of worry, panic, fear, doubt, or anxiety. Maybe even anger, guilt, and animosity regarding how the situation is unfolding. An incident out of your control may have caused you to lose your job - such as inaccurate accusations about your work performance, a great amount of time from work missed due to health care appointments for you or a family member causing an attendance issue or disciplinary action, or an unrealistic workload to which you couldn't keep up. You may have anger at the company or management for not taking care of business to keep the company afloat. You may have resentment on how things are being handled by lawmakers. You may be bitter, insulted, or humiliated because you knew you were at the top of the class in being a loyal and hardworking employee and made personal sacrifices for the sake of the company and for your job. All of these things would be understandable in feeling the way that you may be feeling right now. But here's the thing. All of the emotions and reactions just described are negative.

The things you need now are the focus, energy, a clear heart, and a clear mind. Any negative emotions will do nothing but have you rehearse the pain internally of what happened over and over and keep you in a state of stagnation. Stagnation and rehearsing over and over about what happened in discussion to yourself and to others will not help you secure a new opportunity nor "clear the air" for something good to come your way.

Release Any Grudges

Don't hold grudges. You may not or will not see it now, but you are in a better position. Your value and importance is no longer based upon your job or a position that you hold. You are no longer bound by that way of living and thinking. You are not a has-been or a former employee or executive. You are now an individual developing strength and who is now independent from the label of "I am a 'this'" and "I worked at 'that company'."

Again, negative feelings and thoughts won't get you a job quicker, put money in your pocket faster, help you to keep an open mind on potential income opportunities, or get you rehired - if getting rehired was even a possibility. You sure can't eat off of these feelings and thoughts either - they won't feed you. What you need to do is keep your mind positive and focused on the possibilities and opportunities that exist and show up.

A Bumpy Ride But Worth The Trip

This might not seem like an easy trip. In fact, it may seem a little rough because the journey will be over choppy waters never before seen. But as you travel out the cold dark storm onto the sunny beaches, you'll be back on track with a proper perspective in life and may even ask, "What was the name of that place where I worked again?"

A LIVELIHOOD TRANSITION (LT)

From this point on in this book, any reference to "a job lost", "layoff", "furlough", "termination", "loss in income", etc. (except in the page header for the book title, of course) will be called a Livelihood Transition - LT for short. Transition means to move from one thing or place to another. Livelihood is what you do to financially maintain your household. Those other words such as "layoff" continue the negativity of bitter emotions in a subtle way. The only way to gain is to look for gain and to expect gain - not to look back and dwell upon any notion that there is lack of gain. Even the word "job" is now replaced with livelihood or opportunity. An opportunity opens up a world of possibilities that can't be categorized as a "job".

As hard as this may seem and as crazy as this may sound, celebrate the change. Celebrate the LT. If there were anything that you could have done, you would have done it. If there were any way that your livelihood could have remained the same, it would have happened.

Life has a natural flow and if you flow in it, you'll find yourself in another land BETTER than the land you just left. You **MUST** adjust your outlook immediately toward the positive.

From this point on, spend every millisecond of speech, energy, activity, and focus on being grateful for:

1) The opportunities, the skills, and the experience gained
2) All the people and things in your life that you currently have
3) The great opportunities that are now and in the future

Panic and worry, places one in a state of mind based upon the unknown of the future. Unless you have a crystal ball, you do not know what good or miracle is going to come your way - and for sure you don't want to block anything good from coming your way. Negative energy and emotions have a way of blocking that good.

If you feel sad, angry, or depressed, it's because you are looking at the past. If you are anxious, fearful, doubtful, or worried, you are looking at the future. You can only live and exist in the present. If there is any time to adopt the exercise of faith, it would be now. If you feel or are experiencing any negative emotions, you are not living in the present.

While living in the present, you must continue to rehearse to yourself that all of your needs are met and will be met.

A Helpful Exercise

Having a spiritual practice can prove to be most helpful during an LT especially when receiving collections calls, exploring income opportunities, and having conversations with creditors. Being spiritual includes prayer and meditation. Being spiritual is not the same as being religious. Being spiritual is simply going within you for peace to your heart, mind, body, and soul. If you are anything but calm, cool, collected, and content, you are not operating from the present moment.

Here is a simple exercise that can help you stay centered:

1) Sit in a quiet area and close your eyes.
2) Begin to take slow long deep breaths.
3) Concentrate on the breath coming in and going out.
4) Ignore any movements, sounds, or any other could-be distractions around you.
5) In and out - feel the breath coming in and then going out.
6) Feel the air travel through your nostrils through your throat then filling up your lungs.
7) Feel your breath travel the reverse course as you exhale.
8) Begin repeating to yourself, even if you don't believe these words at first - keep repeating, "All of my needs are met. All of my needs are met."
9) Keep repeating until you are centered in that moment that "Right now, everything is fine, will be fine, and that all needs are met."
10) Take notice if you are focusing in the future or reflecting on the past. Redirect your thoughts to where you are at that present moment...sitting with eyes closed saying, "all of my needs are met."

11) Take an inventory in your mind of where you are at the present while repeating the words "all of my needs are met". Your basic needs are food, shelter, and clothing. If you had a bite to eat, if you are not sitting in the nude with no apparel available, and if you are not sitting on the sidewalk along with your family and belongings, then these needs are met. That's the first accomplished goal. If health, some soap, and some running water are present, then all is well.

A HEALTHY EXPECTATION LEVEL

This following exercise is just as important as you journey through the various steps, actions, and changes during this LT.

You must remember not to count your chickens before they hatch. It is a possibility that the eggs you think you have will never hatch and there is also a possibility that if the eggs in your basket do hatch, they may not appear to be the offspring you were expecting.

Attach no emotion to this journey of your LT. Of course, you want for the best, but the key is not to base your sun, your moon, or your breath on what you are doing. Simply do what it is that you need to do and move on to the next task with your focus on exploring apparent options and discovering new options.

There may be some things that do not turn out as you had originally envisioned or anticipated. This is the time now to keep your attitude elevated. It is also the time to keep your expectation level high but not on what you see and what you think will be the direct outcome to any actions that you take - but to keep your expectation level high that what you are going through is a learning opportunity with several crash courses along the way.

This book cannot give you a timeline on how long it would be to transition to new and great opportunities. The only indication that this book can give is that there will be a journey, which may be of short duration or of which may be a long period of time.

Pride Before the fall

There will be suggestions in this book that may cause one who has always been independent and self-sufficient to feel shameful or feel like a failure if they were to take the suggested action steps.

Pride needs to be removed from the equation. There is nothing too beneath you nor is there anything far above you. Your focus is to maintain and handle business. This is a transitional period and if you maintain the mindset that the transitional period is merely just a season and that a new day is on the horizon, stand tall and walk with your head up high while being grateful there are resources from which you can receive benefits.

If you feel just that embarrassed about using the resources suggested, then just keep it to yourself. If somebody sees you at a program office or at a food pantry, then they just see you. Chances are, they are already in your shoes because they are at the same place because you are looking at them. Also, trust and believe there is something about you or in your life that a person, you would least expect, wish they had in their life - no matter the circumstance.

Do not turn the page until you have adopted and put into practice these principles and first steps.

APPLYING FOR BENEFITS DUE TO UNEMPLOYMENT

The Connection in Services

It is suggested that you apply for all benefits at the same time as most of social service and state agencies are interconnected in obtaining income eligibility and verification of your current status and assets.

You may find that in order to be eligible for cash assistance, medical assistance, and food stamps, you may have to file for unemployment first to determine or establish a new household income amount. However, in order for your children to receive a free or reduced meal plan at school, you may have to have the food stamp assistance established first. Again, each state, county, and school district works differently and you must contact each entity to which you will make application to obtain eligibility criteria and an understanding on the guidelines as to what benefit or programs needs to be in place before proceeding to apply and receive other benefits and programs.

File for Unemployment Compensation Immediately

What is Unemployment Compensation or Unemployment Benefits?

Unemployment Insurance is what employers pay into the state to cover their employees who may become out of work through no fault of the employee. Employees who are out of work due to no fault of their own are typically eligible to receive unemployment compensation or unemployment benefits.

Every state has its own specific guidelines on how unemployment benefits are paid out to eligible out of work employees as well as its own guidelines as to what are the eligibility requirements.

Eligibility requirements are generally based upon:

1) Meeting the minimum number of weeks worked prior to becoming out of work

2) Meeting the minimum average weekly wage as set forth by the state

Usually, the benefit amount is calculated from what the employee earned during a base period. Base periods are typically a one-year period of time with the earliest four of the last five complete quarters of the calendar year. Compensation benefits are not based upon the most recent salary received but based upon what was received during that base period. If the employee worked at more than one employer, wages earned for all employers will be used to determine the average weekly wage.

The following is a base period chart example:

2011	2012				2013			
Oct Nov Dec	Jan Feb Mar	Apr May Jun	Jul Aug Sep	Oct Nov Dec	**Jan Feb Mar**			
	Jan Feb Mar	Apr May Jun	Jul Aug Sep	Oct Nov Dec	Jan Feb Mar	**Apr May Jun**		If Jim files his application in April, May or June of 2013, his base period would be January through December of 2012.
		Apr May Jun	Jul Aug Sep	Oct Nov Dec	Jan Feb Mar	Apr May Jun	**Jul Aug Sep**	If Mary applies in July, August, or September of 2013, her base period would be April of 2012 through March of 2013
			Jul Aug Sep	Oct Nov Dec	Jan Feb Mar	Apr May Jun	Jul Aug Sep	**Oct Nov Dec**

Base Period spans the 2012 quarters.

An alternate base period is used if an out-of-work employee's number of weeks worked did not fall within the base period or the average weekly wage was less than the established minimum within the regular base period. The alternate base period may be another opportunity to be eligible to receive unemployment compensation.

The following is an example of an alternate base period:

2011	2012				2013			
Oct Nov Dec	Jan Feb Mar	Apr May Jun	Jul Aug Sep	Oct Nov Dec	**Jan Feb Mar**			
	Jan Feb Mar	Apr May Jun	Jul Aug Sep	Oct Nov Dec	Jan Feb Mar	**Apr May Jun**		If Jim files his application in April, May or June of 2013, his alternate base period would be April 2012 through March of 2013.
		Apr May Jun	Jul Aug Sep	Oct Nov Dec	Jan Feb Mar	Apr May Jun	**Jul Aug Sep**	If Mary applies in July, August, or September of 2013, her alternate base period would be July of 2012 through June of 2013
			Jul Aug Sep	Oct Nov Dec	Jan Feb Mar	Apr May Jun	Jul Aug Sep	**Oct Nov Dec**

Alternate Base Period spans the 2012 quarters.

Filing for Unemployment Benefits or Compensation

1) File for unemployment compensation with your state immediately either online, in person, or via telephone. If you are unsure about anything in processing your application, it would be better to apply in person or via telephone.

2) Be prepared to give prior year employer information including salary and start/end dates.

3) Be sure to report the number of dependents that you have as there may be a dependency classification formula used to calculate the maximum weekly benefit amount.

4) In your application, you must include any type of business that you own as well as any type of self-employment work that you do.

5) There may be a required waiting period for determination of benefits before the first check is received.

6) Choose to have your compensation direct deposited onto a debit card/pay card/e-card that the unemployment office will issue to you. If you have any pending unsatisfied judgments, it would be wise not to use a personal checking or savings account for this type of compensation.

Keep in mind that the paid benefit may not be anywhere near what your full time salary used to be because unemployment compensation is not designed to replace income and maintain a current lifestyle of living. Unemployment compensation is designed to keep the mere basics going until other opportunities are gained and in place to return the household to financial stability.

Unemployment compensation is considered taxable income, therefore a 1099 tax form will be sent to you to file with your tax return. Unemployment compensation must be reported as income on the appropriate line on the IRS tax form.

If you have any questions regarding tax laws and unemployment compensation, contact a tax attorney, the Internal Revenue Service, and/or your state's Unemployment Office.

Having a Second Position

If you worked a full time position and a part-time position and you are released from the full time position, do not resign from the part-time position. Eligibility to receive unemployment compensation is based on an employee becoming out of work through no fault of his or her own. Resigning from a position, whether it is part-time or not, is a voluntary decision and could possibly make you ineligible to receive unemployment benefits. Continue to report to the part-time position. There **may** be an eligibility component that offers an opportunity to receive some unemployment compensation to offset the loss of the full time position.

Furloughed Employees

Furloughed employees may or may not be eligible for unemployment compensation. Employees that are furloughed should contact their state's unemployment office as soon as possible for eligibility requirements.

If you are an employee that has been given reason to believe that a furlough is imminent, be sure to contact your state's unemployment office as soon as possible BEFORE the furlough begins.

Outside Income While Receiving Unemployment

If you earned money while receiving unemployment benefits, you must report it for the week that it was earned and you will most likely receive a deduction of that amount from your benefits for that week.

For example, Mary receives $400 a week as a weekly unemployment benefit. Mary decided to use the time awaiting an income opportunity between interviews to do consulting work to build a business. Mary contracted with a client that she would work so many hours for the week on a particular project and in return her fee would be $400.

In Mary's state of residence, she is required to report what she has earned for that week whether or not she will actually receive those earnings in that particular week. Because Mary's fee was equal to her weekly benefit, Mary will probably not receive her weekly benefit of $400 for that week. Although Mary made $400, she gained $0 instead of the extra $400 she was counting on. Also, Mary will not see the $400 that she earned until her client pays it to her, thus leaving Mary with no weekly benefit for that week.

If Mary's state allows for a certain percentage of her weekly benefit amount to be exempted from any earnings that she makes, she may receive a reduced weekly benefit.

If Mary's state allowed for 20% of her weekly benefit to be exempted, Mary's calculated earnings deduction could be $320 instead of the original $400 (20% of Mary's weekly benefit of $400 is $80 - subtracting that $80 from the $400 that Mary earned leaving $320). Taking the $320 from her weekly benefit of $400 leaves Mary to receive $80 for that particular week's benefit. Mary did not see a $400 gain for her work efforts, but experienced an $80 gain for the week because of the state's earnings exemption of 20% from her weekly benefit.

Keep in mind, however, that Mary received just $80 for that particular week. When Mary finally receives her fee of $400 from her client, it will presumably be during a week where she receives her weekly unemployment benefit of $400 as well if she is still eligible to claim unemployment benefits.

Again, your state will have specific rules regarding earning income while receiving unemployment benefits. Be sure that you understand the advantages and disadvantages of earning income while receiving unemployment compensation according to your state's guidelines.

Income that must be reported and may be deducted from your weekly benefit includes:

- Severance Pay
- Vacation Pay
- Holiday Pay
- Pensions
- Company Separation Packages
- Workers' Compensation

Income that may not be deducted include:

- Social Security
- Military Reserve Pay (be sure to know the parameters)
- Interest Dividends
- Rental Income

Be sure to examine if your state allows any percentage of your weekly benefit to be exempted from any other income that you receive before a deduction is made.

Travel or Medical Leave During an Unemployment Claim

When receiving unemployment compensation, it may not be an ideal time to travel (either for business or pleasure) or to have healthcare procedures done. Generally, someone receiving unemployment compensation is expected to be available to work. One cannot be available to work when out of town for pleasure, in a hospital bed, or at home convalescing.

However, healthcare is the number one priority and if a procedure needs to be performed, then by all means get it done immediately. Just keep in mind, that while under medical care with no ability to work, your eligibility may change during that time period.

Be sure to study your state's guidelines and contact your state's unemployment office if you have any questions regarding:

- Deductible income
- Non-deductible income
- Traveling out of state
- Earning money while out of state
- Having health care procedures that would normally not allow an immediate return to work
- Receiving lottery, gambling, or contest winnings

Remember: The eye of the prize is to get off of unemployment as soon as possible with a suitable income that will sustain your household, pay off debt, support medical coverage, and build a savings fund.

Cash/Food Stamp Assistance

It may be wise to file for cash and food stamp assistance immediately when filing for unemployment.

However, there could be a thin line in applying too close to receiving your last earned income payment - which may make you ineligible for benefits upon application where you have already received income for the month. Eligibility for benefits depends on your county and state guidelines.

Call your county Human Services offices and:

1) Give them your address. Then ask them to tell you to which office in your city you should go to apply for benefits according to your residential location. Some counties have various offices to serve residents in a certain geographical area so you want to be sure you go to the correct office the first time so that there is no unnecessary delay such as the wrong office sending your application to another office, being directed from the wrong office to visit another office to apply, etc.

2) Also ask them what you need to bring with you to make application and/or to an appointment. Generally these items are:

- Birth certificates (for you and every household member)
- Social security cards (for you and every household member)
- Proof of children's school attendance for any dependents
- Unemployment Determination Letter
- Termination/Lay-Off/Last Day Worked Letter from Employer
- Driver's License
- Mortgage Payment Record/Rent Receipts
- Copy of Current Utility Bills

CHILD SUPPORT

If you received child support for your children, it was probably helpful to your household when having regular income. However, child support can become a hindrance when applying for cash and food stamp assistance, as it may be included while determining eligibility.

The most unfortunate thing is that although child support may be considered income for eligibility determination, child support is not a guaranteed source of income. There may be times when the child support payer may not be able to make payments on time so you will not receive child support for whatever period of time that the payer cannot make the payments. If that were the case, it would be a good idea to contact your caseworker as soon as possible to report the change. Reporting this type of change may cause an increase in benefits and allow your household to be eligible for additional resources.

If you are a payer of child support and you have lost your source of income, you will continue to accrue arrearages to your case support order. You may file for a hearing to have your child support payments adjusted due to financial hardship. You must call your local county child support enforcement agency to receive clear guidelines on the opportunities that you may have given your particular circumstances.

Be sure to keep in mind that a request to have an adjustment may not yield a decreased payment amount if you are the payer. Some adjustment hearings uncover a greater support need for the child resulting in a support order to increase the payment amount.

Note: Always report any change in income into the household to any agency from which you are receiving benefits - whether the change is more income or less.

MEDICAL COVERAGE - COBRA AND APPLYING FOR MEDICAID

COBRA

COBRA stands for the Consolidated Omnibus Budget Reconciliation Act, which became law in 1986. COBRA allows you to extend the same health care coverage and continue to enjoy the benefits of that coverage that you had with your last employer for generally up to 18 months.

But COBRA is not free. In fact, it extends the benefits but transfers all of the cost to you. So if $50 was deducted from your check but the company paid $950 a month for your benefits, your monthly premium payment under COBRA to have and keep those great benefits could cost you $1,000 a month or more.

You have up to 45 days to begin paying your premium payments and when you do, you have to pay for coverage all the way back to the last day that you worked.

Medicaid

Apply for Medicaid when you apply for cash and food stamp assistance if you cannot afford the COBRA payments or any other self-pay payments to continue your medical coverage - especially if you have children. You may be more likely to obtain Medicaid if you have dependents.

Your county Medicaid program may have several healthcare coverage plans from which to choose. Be sure to call your existing medical, dental, and vision providers/doctors to see what healthcare coverage plans that they accept.

Your county or state websites may have a downloadable guide for reduced or free health care service providers that offer medical, dental, and vision care services at a reduced cost, on a sliding pay fee scale according to household income, or at no cost at all. Some of these providers may only schedule new clients on the first day of every month.

Other Sources

Major Hospital Systems - Your city's major hospital systems may offer programs to assist with health care needs. Contact each hospital system and ask to speak with a financial counselor that can advise you if they have programs for which you are eligible. The financial counselor may ask you to provide financial documentation including prior year's tax records and a statement about your income such as an unemployment determination letter, Social Security award letter, etc. Contact all state, county, and city operated hospital systems. Be sure to inquire within every hospital system about any specific programs that are offered through partnerships with other hospital systems or organizations.

Public Health Departments - Contact your county and local public health departments as these governmental departments provide free screenings and care for various health care needs.

Free Clinics - In addition, many metropolitan areas have Free Clinics which are medical facilities offering community healthcare on a free or on a low cost basis.

Affordable Care Act

For more information on the Affordable Care Act and what to do about health care if you are participating in a COBRA plan or receiving Medicaid benefits, go to www.healthcare.gov. Visit the website or call the phone number available on www.healthcare.gov as well as your state and county Human Services departments if:

- You are unsure what to do if you are participating in a COBRA plan or receiving Medicaid benefits
- You are unsure about your state's guidelines or available plans within the Affordable Care Act
- You have questions as to what will happen if your COBRA plan period or Medicaid benefits period is completed and you had not yet selected a Marketplace plan
- You have questions as to the best option from which to choose for healthcare coverage for your particular situation

Contact the Veteran Administration

If you are a Veteran, be sure to contact the Veteran Administration to obtain information about medical care available to veterans.

Healthcare for Everyone

No matter the race, nationality, gender, or tax bracket, every human being deserves quality healthcare.

Some service providers may provide "reduced" treatment and care based on the patient's ability to pay and/or the non-existence of insurance coverage.

Take the time to research for opportunities to receive affordable yet quality health care.

IMPORTANT NOTES ABOUT ANY GOVERNMENT BENEFITS

- If someone in the household is receiving Social Security benefits, all income changes must be reported to Social Security if other household members' incomes were a factor in calculating the Social Security benefit. Be sure to contact your local Social Security Administration office immediately if there is any type of income change.

- Be sure to answer all questions on any and all applications honestly and report any income that you may receive when you file your unemployment claim (as required) or when applying for cash, food and medical assistance. As noted before, most governmental and public programs systems are interconnected. There are systems in place to discover if an applicant is giving false information or has access to resources that was not disclosed. These agency systems are connected with healthcare systems as well as financial institutions.

- Remember that anything that uses a social security number can be tracked.

- If you hold any professional licenses, be sure to report any license reactivations or changes - even if the profession or salary is commission only. By not reporting this activity, it can be looked upon as an intention not to disclose all information truthfully and honestly. If there are commission only opportunities available to you, be sure to note that the salary is based on commission with no method to predict future commission amounts or frequency. When a commission is received or generated, be sure to report it immediately.

- Only list dependents that are truly your dependents.

- Repercussions including up to fines and prosecution could very well result due to falsification in any manner to obtain any type of benefit.

- Falsifying any governmental or financial application is a felony. Having a felony could bring death to the garden of your opportunities. Once you have a criminal record, it could be quite difficult to almost impossible to obtain employment. Most companies do not trust those with felonies around their money, their business resources, employees, or with confidential information.

- It may also prove to be very difficult to obtain state required professional or financial licenses through various agencies or sponsoring companies.

DO NOT COUNT ON ANY GOVERNMENT FUNDED BENEFIT.

Remember: Certain benefits, especially when it comes to Unemployment and Food Stamp Assistance, are a means of temporary assistance and can cease, be reduced, or be denied at any time especially in this season of sequestration, government shut downs, and city, state, and national budget deficits.

Do what you are to do to apply for these benefits. Since any governmental assistance or benefit can cease availability at any time, it is imperative to only place enough energy and focus to begin the application process and to provide all information requested by any case manager or representative of the governmental agency.

Once you have done what you have needed to do, place all of your focus and expectations in doing what you need to do to take care of your household. Do not mark your calendar for when the next benefit amount will be received and do not base your household sustainability on these benefits. Take the steps necessary that you are to take for the benefits of which you are eligible and then move on.

There is no growth or success in aspiring to be a governmental benefit recipient and there is definitely no guarantee of sustainability. However, there are governmental benefits for those who justifiably qualify to receive them on a permanent basis.

Complacency in receiving governmental benefits such as unemployment compensation is like being a survivor of a shipwreck surrounded by sharks while sitting in an inflatable lifeboat that can deflate and sink at any time while the shore is at a far off distance.

GETTING HOUSEHOLD BILLS IN ORDER

The Next Thing To Do Is Make A List

Make a list of every bill with a column for the monthly amount and a column to check if they were paid through automatic debit from a bank account. Then sort them in the expense categories as detailed in this chapter.

The list would look something like this:

Due Date of the Month	Expense	Monthly Payment	Auto Debit Institution
Every Week	Groceries/School Lunch	$140.00	No
1	Mortgage (Taxes and Insurance Included)	$756.00	No
3	Property Taxes	$104.00	Generations Bank of North America
5	Electricity	$70.00	No
7	Land Line Phone	$12.00	Generations Bank of North America
9	Cell Phone	$116.00	Credit Union
10	Appliance Credit Card	$69.00	No
12	Student Loan	$120.00	Credit Union
13	Clothing Credit Card	$98.00	No
16	Gas	$90.00	Generations Bank of North America
19	Car Note	$256.00	No
20	Car Insurance	$66.00	Generations Bank of North America
25	Homeowner's Insurance	$85.00	Credit Union
30	Cable	$108.00	No
30	Internet	$39.00	No

Category 1: Your "Got to Pay" Expenses:

What you pay if nothing else.

Rent/Mortgage - The roof over your head is the absolute top priority. Call your mortgage company (or landlord) **before** you are forced to make a late payment. The mortgage lenders and banking institutions are working closer with homeowners to help them stay in their home more so than in the recent past. Depending on your rent payment history and conduct as a tenant, your landlord MAY work with you and establish a payment plan for you to pay back rent when you get back on your feet.

Utilities (Basics: Electricity, Gas, Water, Land Line) - Basic utilities is what you need to stay warm, bathe, cook your food, make emergency calls, and receive phone calls to set up interviews and social services appointments. Call your utility companies immediately and let them know your situation. You may qualify for a special payment plan or low-income program.

Food and Clothing - Food and clothing go without saying. You can't go hungry or naked.

Transportation (Car Note/Gas/Bus or Train Fare) - You need transportation to get to various interviews and appointments as well as to commute to your new income opportunity. If you feel that you will have difficulty in paying your car note, call the finance company as soon as possible and let them know your situation. They may have payment options and programs to assist you in keeping your car to avoid repossession.

When I called my auto finance company, they offered a program where I could pay my car note weekly via direct debit from my checking account. I did not like that idea for many reasons that will be explained as you read this entire book. However, the most important things were keeping the car and the bottom line cost. The program that they offered me:

- Saved $10 a month wiring fee because it was difficult to raise the entire amount before the due date.
- Saved $12 a month late fee for the same reason as the $10 wiring fee.

- Provided the loan to be paid off slightly earlier than the original loan term and there were no pre-pay penalties.
- Required a $2.00 a month maximum service fee.
- Gave opportunity to maintain a positive credit rating regarding the car loan.

Property Taxes - Your county may have programs available to assist you with a payment arrangement for your property taxes and it is better to pay something toward them because if you do not, it is possible that someone else can pay your delinquent property taxes thus putting a claim on your property, i.e. a Tax Lien Certificate Sale. Be sure to ask your county treasurer if this is a possibility regarding your home/property.

This is a sample list of the "Got to Pay" expenses:

Due Date of the Month	Expense	Monthly Payment	Auto Debit Institution	Category
Every Week	Groceries/School Lunch	$140.00	No	Got to Pay
1	Mortgage (Taxes and Insurance Included)	$756.00	No	Got to Pay
3	Property Taxes	$104.00	Generations Bank of North America	Got to Pay
5	Electricity	$70.00	No	Got to Pay
16	Gas	$90.00	Generations Bank of North America	Got to Pay
19	Car Note	$256.00	No	Got to Pay

Category 2: Your "Try to Pay" Expenses

Auto Insurance, Medical Insurance, and Life Insurance - It is possible that you will not be able to keep your insurance coverage and policies for a moment. You can only do but so much and you have to take care of your basics. For auto insurance, drop down to liability coverage if you cannot afford full coverage (but that depends on if you still have a note on the car). You will need some type of coverage because it would cost you greatly if you don't have coverage versus having at least the minimal coverage that your state dictates. Shop around for a less expensive insurance policy for your car and life insurances. If you cannot afford insurance on your car, then you will have to park your car and use public transportation and remain positive that your car will be okay parked until you can obtain and maintain auto insurance. If you have a car note on your car, be sure to let the auto finance company know about your situation and inability to have insurance coverage.

Options for medical services will be touched upon a little later.

Cell Phone, TV Cable/Satellite Service, and DSL/Internet Service - DSL/Internet service and cell phone service are not basic necessities. They are a close second on the priority list, if you have children with whom you need to keep in contact and in any case of emergencies - especially if you have digital phone service that requires Internet connection.

It would be more convenient to sit up at home in loungewear and search for income opportunities, but you may need to say goodbye to your monthly DSL bill, get up, shower, dress and go to the library every day to search the websites and check your e-mail for responses to applications.

If your personal e-mail address is tied to your DSL service, create a free e-mail address through any of the major website search engines immediately. Use that addresses as your contact address at the beginning of your search in the slight chance that you may lose your DSL service down the road.

There are some major Internet service provider companies that offer discounted rates or special programs for households that meet a certain income level eligibility requirement. Be sure to look into these possibilities and make inquiries.

The following is a sample list of the "Try to Pay" expenses:

Due Date of the Month	Expense	Monthly Payment	Auto Debit Institution	Category
7	Land Line Phone	$12.00	Generations Bank of North America	Try to Pay
9	Cell Phone	$116.00	Credit Union	Try to Pay
20	Car Insurance	$66.00	Generations Bank of North America	Try to Pay
30	Internet	$39.00	No	Try to Pay

Category 3: Your "Just Can't Pay Right Now" Expenses:

Student Loans
Back Taxes
Medical Bills
Credit Cards
Old Debt

These are the bills that may just have to be put on hold after proper attention is given to them.

Student loan lenders may offer unemployment and financial hardship deferment programs. Enroll in those programs immediately. Though the interest may continue to accrue until the loans are paid off, you will have a moratorium from making monthly payments and your credit will not be gravely affected during the deferment time period.

Call the IRS and explain your situation and take opportunity to follow the programs that they prescribe that our available to you.

Call your state and city tax authorities if you have back taxes and explain your situation. There may be a minimum amount that they can accept from you if you have earned income (income other than unemployment and child support). It is possible that your tax refund may be seized to pay back taxes depending on how long you have owed those taxes.

Consult an attorney in your state to determine if unemployment and child support can be garnished to pay federal, state, and city back taxes.

If you don't have the money, then you just don't have the money to pay old medical bills, credit cards, and other old debt. Refer to the "The Bill Collectors" chapter of this book for next action steps.

This is a sample list of the "Just Can't Pay Right Now" expenses:

Due Date of the Month	Expense	Monthly Payment	Auto Debit Institution	Category
10	Appliance Credit Card	$69.00	No	Just Can't Pay Right Now
12	Student Loan	$120.00	Yes	Just Can't Pay Right Now
13	Clothing Credit Card	$98.00	No	Just Can't Pay Right Now
25	Homeowner's Insurance	$85.00	Credit Union	Just Can't Pay Right Now
30	Cable	$108.00	No	Just Can't Pay Right Now

Cancel ALL Automatic Debits and Internet Bank Payment Schedules

The first thing you need to do regarding all of your bank accounts is to cancel every single automatic debit payment and internet banking scheduled payments that you had authorized or that you created to be deducted from your bank account in the order of due date. Do not wait until you have received your last paycheck or severance/vacation payment.

In case you may not have known, a returned item or bounced check can be an automatic bank charge ranging from $19 to $50 if you do not have an insufficient fund or overdraft protection plan attached to your bank account and/or the funds to support that type of program if so required. If that bank charge results in your account ending in a negative balance, the bank will soon begin (in a matter of days) charging a daily overdraft fee ranging from $5 to $10.

Example

Returned Item (amount of payment/original price) $19.95

Returned Item Bank Fee: $39.00

Daily Overdraft Fees for 30 Days (avg. $8/daily): $240.00

In a month's time:
The $19.95 payment/debit now costs you $298.95!!

One missed payment and the bank fees will mount up beyond your ability to catch up in the near future even if you obtain an income opportunity in a short manner of time. Plus, why would you want to pay hundreds of dollars to a bank because of a bounced check or returned item when the original cost was only $19.95?

Be sure to cancel the automatic debit accounts and Internet banking payment schedules as soon as you learn there will be a momentary change in your income. Sometimes it takes some companies' financial department several days to a couple of weeks to cancel an automatic debit. You especially do not want to be debited for a bill payment that falls under the "Try to Pay" or "Just Can't Pay Right Now" expenses.

On the following page is a sample list of the bills that were paid using an automatic debit set-up:

Due Date of the Month	Expense	Monthly Payment	Auto Debit Institution	Category
3	Property Taxes	$104.00	Generations Bank of North America	Got to Pay
7	Land Line Phone	$12.00	Generations Bank of North America	Try to Pay
9	Cell Phone	$116.00	Credit Union	Try to Pay
12	Student Loan	$120.00	Credit Union	Just Can't Pay Right Now
16	Gas	$90.00	Generations Bank of North America	Got to Pay
20	Car Insurance	$66.00	Generations Bank of North America	Try to Pay
25	Homeowner's Insurance	$85.00	Credit Union	Just Can't Pay Right Now

1 + 1 = 2

No matter what is on the "Got to Pay" expense list, the total monthly expense amount has to be less than the total income amount coming into the home. The only way around that is to increase the income coming in, take line items off of the list, or make arrangements to lower the payment amount if at all possible.

While making these mathematical adjustments, it may be necessary to drop a "Got to Pay" expense to the "Try to Pay" expense or to drop a "Try to Pay" expense to a "Just Can't Pay Right Now" expense.

The numbers have to add up and there must not be any chicken counting before the eggs hatch. If you are expecting some type of money outside of any severance money or unemployment compensation, don't count on it until it is in hand and then don't count on it for the next go round.

Also, remember if receiving unemployment compensation, earned income may not actually be extra income if your state deducts what you make from the payment benefit.

YOUR BANK ACCOUNTS

Close All Bank Accounts Except One

Close all banking accounts that charge a monthly maintenance fee. If all of the accounts charge monthly maintenance fees then keep just the one account open that offers the most benefits and services.

The one remaining bank account is used as a temporary holding account for making online utility payments or a special debit payment plan for one of your "Got to Pay" expenses.

This action is to eliminate all unnecessary expenses and to keep your money safe as much as possible with concentration on one bank account. You could possibly have so many things going on that you may have missed something to come through by not keeping your bank account reconciled.

Check Cashing With Existing Judgments

If you need to cash a check, do not deposit it into your bank account as those funds would not be exempt from garnishment.

Instead, there are many check cashing locations that will cash government or employment checks for a nominal fee or percentage. If the check is a personal check, go to the bank printed on the check. You may be charged a non-customer check-cashing fee but you will be certain that the check is good.

Keep in mind that our world is linked through databases. I found a check-cashing center in my area and the check-cashing fee was less than $5. However, I noticed that when they entered my social security number, they were able to pull up a former name and previous addresses. I decided not to use that check-cashing center for any type of payroll check because I did not know, nor could the cashier tell me, if the payroll information from cashing the check was being recorded and reported.

The information in this chapter is based upon my own understanding and experiences and in no way serves as legal advice. Consult an attorney for legal advice regarding full details of the garnishment process including exemptions from garnishment, protecting your money and your legal rights. If you cannot afford an attorney, contact your city, county, and state for attorneys that assist clients free of charge or at a reduced rate and/or obtain a legal services membership.

FINDING INCOME OPPORTUNITIES

Expectations Checkpoint

You have applied for all of the major programs and services available to you. This is where you must check your expectations level. If you are expecting for the major programs and services to "take care of you", you are setting yourself for quite possibly a great disappointment.

Eligibility is on a case-by-case basis. Where you might would believe that you would be eligible, you may obtain a denial letter instead of an approval letter. If you receive a denial letter, there should be an opportunity to file for an appeal on the decision. If there is or if there is not an opportunity to appeal, the most important thing is to maintain an appropriate level of focus or energy to any one task.

Do not let any setbacks become a setback to your positive attitude nor a drain to your positive energy or focus. Remember negative feelings and a negative outlook does nothing to serve anybody including any of the members you may have in your household.

To maintain a healthy expectation level during this LT is to remember and practice the exercises and maintain the healthy expectation level introduced in the chapters "First Things First" and "A Livelihood Transition."

Register with Every Employment and Temporary Agency In Your City

More and more companies are using employment agencies to fill position openings within their organization either via direct placement or via temporary or contracted term assignments. Companies use employment agencies to save the time and expenses in soliciting and recruiting talent for their organizations.

The employment agencies perform all the legwork in the screening and interviewing process to reap the best of the crop to present to the company for consideration. The recruiting or employment agencies want to keep the companies as clients so the agencies are going to make sure they present nothing but the best of the best.

Companies also choose to recruit contract employees through an agency to eliminate their costs of covering health care and other benefits for the employee. The employment agencies are then responsible for employee benefit offerings as well as other labor related responsibilities such as unemployment compensation.

Seek out employment agencies that only charge placement and services fees to the company and not to the individual seeking an income opportunity.

Employment agencies place people in:

- **Temporary Positions** - the duration being anywhere from a day to a year or more with no promise of being hired by the company where you are assigned. The assignment ends on the date specified on the contract including assignment extensions.

- **Temp to Perm Positions** - these assignments are so the company can see how well you can perform the tasks and how well you get along with other team members before they make the investment to hire you on full time.

- **Direct Hire Positions** – these placements are when companies use an agency as their recruiting department to find people to be hired as a regular employee who would be eligible for company benefits depending if the selected candidate is on a full time or part-time status.

Employment agencies recruit in every industry and in every position from CEO to general laborer. The following are the usual steps to register with an employment agency:

- Call the agency.

- The staffing specialist at the employment agency schedules an appointment with you to come in and interview.

- The staffing specialist will want an updated resume to send to potential employers and may offer suggestions on how to improve the content or appearance of your resume to attract their clients' attention if your skills or experience meet the criteria of a particular position.

- The interview will consist of questions for the staffing specialist to learn: what are your strengths and weaknesses, your availability, what type of work you would like to do, as well as your minimum salary requirement.

- The employment agency may have a battery of tests for you to complete to assess your skills.

- The staffing specialist will tell you what the employment agency currently has available while submitting your name and resume to potential opportunities that best match your skills and/or the staffing specialist will place you on their availability or candidate lists for future opportunities.

Due to the transitions that the economy seems to be experiencing and/or during the time of year, there may be some quiet seasons for the employment/temporary agencies where you may not hear from them for weeks to months. This is why it is important to register with every agency that fills positions in the industry where you are experienced and desire to work.

As soon as you believe it was a waste of time to register with multiple agencies, the phone could start ringing with multiple opportunities for your name and resume to be submitted for a position resulting in an assignment or regular full-time employment.

Employment agencies generally do not advertise upfront the name of the company who is seeking to fill the position. They usually do not divulge the name of the company until the company has had the opportunity to review the candidate pool that the agency submits for consideration. Only the candidates who the company wishes to interview are told the company name, location, and contact information.

There are legitimate fee placement agencies that will charge you a fee to assist you in a customized job search. Do not use these types of agencies unless you have quite a bit of a nest egg to maintain your household's current expenses during a year of an LT. It would be wise to use a fee placement agency when you already have a position and are ready to advance. You should hopefully at that time have the resources to pay for their services.

The Pros and Cons of Employment/Temporary Agencies

Pros:

- Companies use these types of agencies to recruit for open positions within their organization that they would not otherwise advertise to the public.

- You have an opportunity to work as a temporary in an organization to learn the culture. You may not like the position or the company and that would be a plus if you are there for a temporary period of time. Every person is not a fit for every employment opportunity and every employment opportunity is not a fit for every person.

- You have the opportunity to learn and develop new skills while meeting new people at a faster pace than if you were permanently employed at one location.

- If crafted creatively, your resume will detail experience in various industries and positions – making your services marketable.

Cons:

- For temporary and temp to perm assignments, medical insurance is not company-paid and you may have to pay for insurance at a higher premium through the agency, more so than if you were employed full time by the company where you were placed. However, due to the Affordable Care Act, there may be additional available options to have healthcare coverage for you and your dependents.

- If the assignment turns out not to be a good fit and the assignment is terminated before the contracted end date, the agency may not continue to work with you to find another assignment. Also, the employment agency may not agree to pay unemployment compensation.

- You may find yourself with a strong desire to be full time but that opportunity may not work out that way. There is the possibility of an emotional detachment period from the position and from the new relationships that were created if the company is not hiring full time and your assignment ends.

- It could be a mental and emotional drain every few months to learn a new job and a new company as well as its culture, procedures, and employee personalities.

- If not crafted creatively, your resume will show sporadic work experience. This may give the potential employer an impression that you are unstable or not worthy of full-time hire with so many temporary assignments. The employer may begin to wonder why weren't you hired on as a full-time employee in the previous temporary opportunities and then move on to select a candidate with a more stable work history.

Accept Long Term Employment Assignments While Within An Unemployment Benefit Period

Be sure to accept an assignment that is longer than the required number of weeks to work to be eligible for unemployment.

For example, Mary is receiving unemployment and accepts an assignment that is to last no more than four weeks. In Mary's state, an employee must have worked six weeks at a new place of employment to receive unemployment benefits. Mary may not be eligible for unemployment compensation after completing the four-week work assignment.

Assignments Worth Accepting

Only accept an assignment that is worth accepting. Do not accept an assignment that will not help you to carry your household expenses. It would be tempting to accept an opportunity to work in a temp to hire type assignment at a company to which you've always wanted to work at a salary less than your pre-determined minimum. However, there is no guarantee that you will be hired and accepting a wage or salary that is less than what you need for your particular household may cause you to become further behind in your bills in the long run and may also affect the unemployment compensation benefit amount for the next base period.

Strive to only accept assignments that make mathematical and logical sense as it pertains to income including commuting and parking costs as well.

EMPLOYMENT RESOURCES

Go to the library or search on your county and state websites about state and county sponsored employment resources. Both the state and county have websites that capture all available employment opportunities for that entire region.

Your state may also require you to register with their employment search program in order to continue receiving unemployment benefits. Be sure to follow their guidelines and read immediately all communications that the Unemployment Office sends to your attention.

Your local library systems may have a career counseling center that provide resources regarding resume development, employment search techniques, as well as a list of current available employment opportunities.

It is almost impossible to uncover every service or program available that may be of assistance as you are going through an LT because there are countless programs and services for adults and children ranging from:

- Educational opportunities
- Scholarships
- Food and meal programs
- Reduced or free utility bill programs including internet access
- Rent and mortgage assistance (but be sure to examine these types of programs especially if requested to give personal/confidential information or any fee amounts as some have proven to be scams)
- Clothing and footwear assistance
- Home appliance assistance

Never cease to explore resources from surrounding communities; non-profit organizations including churches; vocational organizations; youth, men, women, and Veteran programs; economic advancement organizations; minority organizations, etc.

Online Employment Posting Boards - Pros and Cons

What better way to seek out employment opportunities than to sit in the comforts of home on a computer versus hitting the pavement going door to door as people did in the recent past. There are many employment websites where you can visit to obtain information about available openings. There are also various online boards specific to industries such as:

- Hospitality
- Pharmaceutical
- Information Technology
- Health Care
- Executive Level Opportunities
- Culinary
- And the list goes on

These websites are a great source to obtain names of employment agencies and to create customized searches and e-mail alerts for opportunities that are specific to what you are seeking.

However, in today's digital age, one must be conscience of best practices about using online posting boards and submitting personal or confidential information over the Internet.

Posting Resume for Public View by Potential Hiring Managers

Some posting boards offer the opportunity for potential hiring managers to review publicly posted resumes of available candidates in their particular industry.

For privacy and security purposes, create a copy of your resume specific for public posting. In the resume that you post publicly, delete your residence address and just post your phone number.

Do not use any mailing addresses including any post office boxes you may have. Do not use any email addresses as well to minimize the opportunity for spam. You do not know who will be reviewing your resume thus you do not want to divulge all of your personal business for anyone to review. Limiting the contact information will not keep you from being contacted from someone who is a serious hiring manager and truly looking for qualified candidates such as yourself. If you make your e-mail address and postal address viewable to the public, it is probable that the majority of contacts you receive will not be actual employment opportunities.

Apply Online Directly on Company Websites

After learning about an opportunity on an online board and the company's name and address are specified, apply for that opportunity directly on that company's website, if possible, to ensure that it is a legitimate opportunity and so that the company will actually receive your application.

Other Entities That Use Online Boards

Insurance Companies - Some insurance companies look to online boards to recruit insurance agents. Although there are fees that licensed professionals must pay to practice, to maintain their licenses in databases, for associations, and/or for continuing education, be especially careful of accepting opportunities that require you to take a loan to begin marketing their insurance plans. Be sure that you fully understand the financial commitment that you are making and that it fits into your current financial spending plan. There aren't too many companies, if any that would indicate that potential earnings would be poor so don't get caught up into the promise and presentational diagrams of great earning potential. When it comes to sales, there are too many different factors on a case-by-case basis to guarantee an earning potential. Do not sign up for any type of financial commitment unless you have a sizable nest egg to fund the commitment and to maintain all of your household and financial obligations.

Network Marketers - Network marketers use employment websites to get contact information of individuals who are looking for a source of income. Network marketing company representatives will call to invite you to an "opportunity meeting" to learn about their product and compensation program. The "opportunity meetings" could be in a conference room, a restaurant, or via phone or videoconferencing.

Network marketing can be an alternative to earn money if you have the entrepreneurial spirit within you. It is not your typical 9 to 5 type of work environment. It takes the dedicated and "hungry" individual to be successful in that type of business and generally requires a lot of hard work. Income is rarely predictable or stable in network marketing, especially in the first one to three years. However, if the personal organization has experienced consistent growth, the earning potential could very well stabilize and become quite lucrative.

Scam Artists - Scam artists use employment websites to prey on the emotions and vulnerability of someone seeking employment with the lure of an imminent employment opportunity. The real goal of the scammer is to guide the unsuspecting employment seeker through a series of questions to get private information such as their social security and bank account numbers. Never put your full social security number or banking information on an online employment application and never send it via e-mail if requested to do so.

Casting Agencies - If you are interested in modeling or acting, be especially careful about agents or agency directors asking for money upfront. Scam artists generally try to play on your emotion by showing you how they can make your dreams come true. Once you are on Cloud 9 you may get caught up in the dream and not stay focused on handling business. Typically, if someone asks you for money for any type of package or program, it would be better to err on the side of being overly cautious and not provide any banking information whatsoever. If the first or last thing out of anybody's mouth is to ask you for money, take a pass on the opportunity no matter how they persist in telling you otherwise. Most legitimate agencies or agents are paid when the artist/actor is paid.

Marketing Leads for Educational Institutions - Keep an eye out on marketing companies and higher learning recruiting services when exploring employment opportunities. The marketing companies generate leads from the people who apply to positions that they have created and posted on the website. Once you have submitted your application, you will be contacted about enrolling into an educational or employment search program that will cost money with the promise that it will help you land an employment opportunity or help you find a better position than for what you are currently qualified. It may take several times to tell a company to stop contacting you. If that company persists, contact the Better Business Bureau, an attorney, and/or any other appropriate governmental entity.

If you are interested in pursuing further education, carefully investigate these types of companies and institutions. If you are only interested in seeking employment, do not let these types of companies or calls deter you from your focus.

Bill Collectors - It is possible that clever bill collectors may comb employment sites to get updated information about the individuals from whom they need to collect. Be sure not to include any self-employment or current temporary agency information on your resume as that will give the bill collectors additional information from where to garnish if they should seek to obtain a judgment against you.

Online Personal and Professional Social Networks - Online social networks are great ways to let people that you personally know that you are looking for employment or income opportunities.

There are also various business networks where you can detail your prior work history, educational background, and skills. Potential employers sometimes use these networks to look for talent for their organizations. However, it would still be in your best interests to be careful about what you post online on any social media platform.

Again, be mindful that bill collectors, as well as stalkers, may visit online posting boards and social networks in search of seeking publicly posted information. Continue to monitor what you publicly display about your professional and personal life.

Your Personal Information

Online applications should only ask for:

- Contact information (mailing address, phone numbers, and e-mail address)
- Work experience
- Educational background
- Certifications/Licenses
- Skills

When you are asked for information other than what is listed above, it is possible that you have embarked on a position that does not truly exist. If it is a marketing ploy or an attempt to get information to be used for identity theft, you will be strung along until you realize that you have been strung along and finally put an end to the farce.

Be sure that you are applying online to legitimate and verifiable companies. If a company's website looks professionally designed with fancy graphics, it's not a legitimate open company if it does not have a real working phone number or verifiable address listed on its website. If the only way to contact the company is via an online fill-in form, than an eyebrow or both should be raised.

Accepting The Right Opportunity

It may be tempting to accept the first income opportunity offer that comes your way. You may feel that a better offer might not come along and you better "get it while you can get it."

Do not accept an offer just because it is the first to come along.

Be sure to accept an offer that will:

- Cover at least the total of the "Got to Pay" expenses AND the "Try to Pay" expenses
- Present an imminent opportunity for advancement with a higher income level to be able to cover the "Just Can't Pay Right Now" expenses as well and allow for savings, healthcare coverage, retirement funding, and future investments
- Not be significantly less than what your skills and experience are worth

For example, Jim was a Project Manager making $52,000 a year before he was laid off. Jim received a call from an employment agency for an opportunity to be a Project Manager making $32,000 a year. Jim's "Got to Pay" and "Try to Pay" expenses total $29,905 a year. Jim is currently receiving unemployment that would equate to $30,000 a year if he received that benefit for the entire year.

When Jim first applied for unemployment, he told the intake worker that the minimum salary that he would accept was $40,000 a year. Jim needs to stick to that amount and not accept anything lower.

When Jim indicated that $40,000 would be the minimum he would accept, Jim was realistic about two things:

1) With the current economy, it may be difficult to get back to the level of an annual salary of $52,000 or more
2) $40,000 would still allow for him to cover all of his expenses while Jim fine tunes his spending habits

Jim knows that unemployment compensation is based on prior income amounts earned. Should Jim accept a significantly lower position today but then down the line two or three years later finds himself in another LT, the unemployment compensation benefit may equate to considerably less than the $30,000 benefit he is currently receiving when he elected to take the $32,000 a year position.

Never settle or allow yourself to be talked into accepting anything less than the standard or limit to which you initially set. This rule could actually be applied to any circumstance.

FOOD AND CLOTHING RESOURCES

Search your city for food pantries, hunger relief centers, and churches that serve free meals. These locations offer an opportunity to pick up food items and feed yourself and/or your family until you obtain food stamp assistance, when you run out of food stamp assistance, or when you do not have eligibility for anything.

If you have seasonal clothing needs for you or your family, search for outreach programs, non-profit organizations/agencies, as well as charitable organizations that provide free or very inexpensive clothing. In addition, search your city for every consignment shop, thrift store, or apparel store that sells slightly used clothing that is in good shape for nominal costs.

Don't pass by or ignore the major department stores and apparel shops in your area. These types of merchants are excellent resources for clothing as well. Some of these establishments offer clothes at ridiculous sales prices where you may find a line of sweaters that were originally marked from $100 to a $1 in the clearance rack just because the store wants to get the sweaters out of inventory. For a family of five, those originally $100 priced sweaters could mean two brand new high-end sweaters for each family member for a total of $10.

YOUR DREAM LIVELIHOOD

Get a journal or notebook and start jotting down what you would love to do as livelihood and/or the names of the companies where you would like to work. Next start jotting down the types of opportunities that you would like to have. Review this list often and pursue these options as your next income opportunity. Share these options with employment agencies, if appropriate, as well as contacting industry specific entities.

For example, if you have always been interested in assisting people with travel arrangements, seek out information about education and experience requirements from travel agencies.

If you have always wanted to work in the medical field, begin contacting educational institutions and healthcare institutions to obtain training and certification requirements as well as timelines, program descriptions, and costs.

Keep your options open and visit the websites of attractive companies on a frequent basis i.e. either twice a week, every Tuesday, but no less than once a week.

Explore companies in various industries including:

- Banking
- Utilities
- Medical and Health Care
- Colleges/Universities
- Local Transportation Services
- Manufacturing
- Pharmaceutical

Begin to bookmark your favorite sites and create a folder designated solely for employment search websites. Then, begin a log, notebook or a spreadsheet with four columns:

Company	Website Address	User Login	Password

The log will help you keep track of how to log in to each site as you build your company list. This type of log is also a good idea to have as a separate file for all of your user ids and passwords for personal accounts as well.

Print out or make a copy of the position description for every opening to which you apply. It may be weeks or months later when the company calls you in for an interview. The description will help you remember for what it was that you applied and will better prepare you to share highlights about your skills and experience that match that particular position.

You will also find that you will begin applying multiple times to one particular company. There may be companies to which you have applied to 15 or 30 open positions.

This is your opportunity to do something that fits into the dreams and visions that you have or may have had in your life. This is an opportunity to explore something that you were predestined to do and be.

Employment specialists may suggest that you study the labor trends. It is okay to investigate and be familiar with what are the growing or "hot" employment opportunities, but don't base your next step on these trends. Base your next step on what you wish to do.

Important Note: If you feel that you are not qualified for the dream career that you want, erase that notion. The only day that you will not be able to obtain the experience and education for what you wish to do is the day when your body temple ceases to function. Anybody can do anything that they want to do if they have the tenacity to do what they need to do to achieve it. Life is limitless so if you can visualize it, it can come to pass.

YOUR DREAM LIFE

Now is the time to truly brainstorm where you desire to spend the majority of your day to earn income. Explore what you would enjoy doing as your livelihood if money was no object. Realize your strengths and weaknesses and create a list of things you would do for a living, but would be happy doing for no pay.

This brainstorm is not about getting an employment opportunity. This brainstorm is about what you dreamed about before your mind was programmed to go to college, enlist in the military, go to vocational school, or become an employee to support yourself because "it was the mature thing to do."

That hobby or dream could be your next step to financial freedom. What have seemed like part-time positions to some have turned out to be lucrative endeavors. Pet taxi services, house sitters, personal shoppers, mobile barbers, dog breeder, cosmetology specialists, writers, bloggers, etc.

When you were a young child and sat on the porch, laid on your bed, or played in the yard, what did you visualize yourself as doing when you became grown? Was it owning a business? Helping people?

When you were a child and people asked you what you were going to be when you grow up, what did you say? Was it a doctor, a nurse, a fireman, a policeman, a superhero? The first four positions are super-heroic in themselves.

The only thing that can stop you from doing what you want to do in life is you. All the other factors can be worked around.

POSSIBILITY A, B, C, D ALL THE WAY TO Z

This is your time to find your own drumbeat and march to it. If you feel you are too old to do something, ask yourself if those are your real feelings or are those feelings that have been influenced by someone or something else - feelings of what you think others might think or say. If you will be 50 years old in four years by the time you obtain a degree or build your business to a profit machine, you'll still be 50 years old in four years. It will be up to you if you will or will not have the degree or business.

It is quite possible that your last place of employment was Plan A instead of Possibility A and that was pretty much it. An LT is an opportunity to run through the alphabet and line up various interests into multiple possibilities.

Possibility B can be to start a cleaning business...and how to start a cleaning business? Work for an office cleaning business on the evenings and weekends while learning the trade and operations. Soon you will have a crew with contracts across the city or region.

Possibility C could be to become a communications technician...and how to start working as a communications technician? Study how that particular technology works or obtain a contract position as a cable installation technician helper and learn on the job.

Possibility D could be to become an author...and how to start working as an author? Start writing. Start off small by writing a page a day and then two pages a day until after so many days you have written volumes. While writing, study how to get published or how to self-publish your own works.

Possibility E could be to start a restaurant chain. Possibility F could be to be a real estate investor or start a real estate brokerage firm. Possibility G could be to open up a chain of chic salons or boutiques. Possibility H could be to become a manufacturer or service provider to fill a niche that no one else has uncovered.

There is no limit to envisioning possibilities. There is nothing ambitious or greedy about it. It's about exercising your full potential and utilizing the gifts and talents that you were given to use.

Keep this in mind and reprogram your thinking to free yourself from the prison of popular and safe opinion. To do you, you have to be you. If you feel there may be a naysayer in the crowd, then keep your possibilities to yourself away from that naysayer and meditate on your dreams and visions as you carry out each step to grow your possibilities into opportunities.

There may be some possibilities that do not pan out. That is perfectly fine. Why? Because you'll have multiple options on the table. It takes blazing through the learning opportunities to get to true success.

BILL COLLECTORS

After you have sorted out your bills in the categories described in the chapter "Get All Your Household Bills In Order", call all of your creditors in priority order and let them know your situation. This will not keep them from calling you. They will call you all through the day, evening, and on weekends. You've told them over and over about your situation and yet they will call the next day like you've never spoken to them ever in life. That's the game that they play to bring you down.

Never forget that: They are debt collectors. Any information that they obtain will be used for that purpose.

When you speak with them or when they call, share only the following:

- You are currently unemployed.

- You cannot make any payment arrangements without having any income.

- Yes, you receive unemployment and it is to pay the mortgage/rent and to buy food for you and/or family (or tell them that you are not receiving unemployment if applicable).

- Yes, you are looking for income opportunities.

- No, you will not borrow the money from anybody and if you did, it would be to pay for the mortgage/rent or to buy food.

- You will not use credit cards or get a payday loan to transfer debt or to get into more debt.

- You are aware that you owe the debt but you are not in the position to pay anything at the present time and cannot and will not go hungry and homeless to do so.

- Tell them to send a statement.

- Do not feel you have to sit and listen to their lectures.

- Do not get threatened or feel intimidated. Hang up the phone if they become rude or disrespectful.

- Hang up the phone if they keep asking you something that you have already addressed.

- Do not give them any of your banking information or tell them anything else about your personal circumstances other than you are unemployed. They do not care about your sob stories. They've been trained to pretend to care or soften you up in hopes that you'll let out some information that they will use later or make a payment commitment to get money from you.

- If you are working part-time, do not tell them that you are working part-time. Also, do not tell them with what company you have made application or have had an interview.

After the initial communication, do the following:

- Write them a letter letting them know about your current financial circumstances (sample letter is included at the end of the book).

- Include the account number, monthly payment amount, and balance due in the letter.

- State in the letter that you will revisit with them in 30 days and every 30 days thereafter until you can resume payments once you obtain steady income again. If this is a creditor for your home or car, you may also let them know that you are in the process of aggressively seeking income opportunities and restructuring your financial situation, but this is optional.

- Keep a log and record of all communications to each creditor.

As long as you are sincere about your intention to pay and demonstrate your intention, some creditors and bill collectors will work with you. Though they are doing their job, the collectors are all still aware about reported economic trends and know that they cannot squeeze juice out of a turnip.

The Bill Collection Process

- The original creditor continues trying to collect.
- The account is turned over to a collections department or company.
- The collections department/company gets stronger in their language and communication attempts to collect the debt.
- The collections department keeps the account for a certain period of time before the original creditor begins court actions for judgment.
- Court actions begin and a court notice is sent.
- If the court notice is not answered within a set period of time, the creditor gets their judgment at the court hearing that is scheduled.
- If the court notice is answered within the specific time period, the judgment is delayed.
- The creditor's attorney can now subpoena personal information such as current employer, current residence address, and so on as well as any documentation that the debtor may have to show that the judgment amount sought is incorrect.
- If it cannot be proven that the creditor is inaccurate regarding the amount due to them, the judgment is rendered and the creditor is able to garnish wages and place liens on property.
- After a payment arrangement cannot be reached or is not maintained, the creditor then issues a Notice of Court Proceeding to Collect Debt. If the debtor is employed, the debtor must complete the calculation worksheet, including all salary and employment information, and send the payment amount as calculated on the form along with the form to avoid garnishment.

- If the debtor does not send in the calculation worksheet along with the payment amount, then the creditor will contact the employer directly to begin garnishment.

Most companies are able to find out where a debtor is currently employed.

I have personally answered two court notices. I looked up a sample of a court answer and put it in the legal document format that would be acceptable to the court. The first court answer prolonged the court proceedings until I was able to get the money up to pay the debt before it became a judgment.

The second court notice that I answered prolonged the case, but it gave opportunity to the creditor to subpoena me for information regarding my current employment, banking and residential information. I knew the job was going to be eliminated because the agency was a non-profit and had experienced a tremendous funding loss. I also knew that I was going to be moving soon. The information that they were able to forcefully obtain legally would soon be no longer valid.

The collection process just previously described is based upon my personal experience and in no way serves as legal advice. Consult an attorney for legal advice regarding full details of the collection process and your legal rights. If you cannot afford an attorney, contact your city, county, and state for a list of attorneys that assist clients free of charge and/or at a reduced rate or you may wish to obtain a legal services membership.

The Creditor's Entitlement To Their Money

You've played the game and delayed judgment, but the courtroom judge's gavel has struck. An entry in the docket and on your credit report shows that you owe an entity a certain amount of money and they can come after you any way they want to get it. That's reality and it's only right. If you owe them, then you have to pay them. Unfortunately, you still can't afford to pay them if you are still going through an LT.

If you have a home, they will put a lien on your property. If you rent, you have nothing for them on which to put a lien, but it's a big problem when you get your income back on track and want to rent elsewhere or finance a home or vehicle. You may have to satisfy that judgment first and wait another year to be able to obtain financing at decent rates.

In the meantime, the collection process begins again. They have permission to snatch a percentage of your wages. They will also be able to probe all into your business by conducting a debtor's examination through the legal system to subpoena you to provide your current residential, banking, employment, and other related information.

Once, I had received a judgment for the last month's rent from two apartments before. I happened to call my landlord about a maintenance matter and she told me that the property management company who had the judgment sent her a letter wanting to know what banking and employer information I had given on my application. Luckily, the information that I gave was no longer valid because I had lost the job that I had when I moved in and I no longer had bank accounts because they were all closed either voluntarily or involuntarily.

The property management company was on a hunt but their actions let me know that they had additional ways to find out information no matter how private I thought I was keeping my business. With the advent of technology, anybody can find you if they looked hard enough.

Payment Arrangements

When the creditors get their judgment, now it's time to make the payment arrangement. But you can't make a payment arrangement on something that you cannot afford. Only, and I repeat only, make a payment arrangement for no more than the dollar amount that you can adjust from your "Got to Pay" expenses. 1 + 1 still equals 2.

If the credit happens to be able to seize a bank account where you have unemployment and/or child support funds coming in, contact an attorney and the bank immediately. Keep in mind, that it could take up to and over a month to release and return these funds to you.

The information in this chapter is based upon my own understanding and in no way serves as legal advice. Consult an attorney for legal advice regarding full details of the garnishment process including funds that are exempt from garnishment as well as your legal rights. If you cannot afford an attorney, contact your city, county, and state for a list of attorneys that assist clients free of charge or at a reduced rate. You may wish to obtain a legal services membership.

EDUCATIONAL OPPORTUNITIES

When an income is not at the ideal level, many can feel that obtaining education or training is impossible for the time being.

There are many educational opportunities available from which to take advantage during an LT.

As of initial publication of this book, The United States Department of Labor Employment and Training Administration has a website with links to various resources from which to begin searching for education and employment programs specific for you. In addition, other helpful links are available on how to find employment, how to maintain a household during a livelihood transition, and knowing your rights as a worker.

Your local, county, and state should have skills training and enhancement programs especially for those who are currently receiving unemployment. Places to contact to learn more about available resources in your area would be your local Health and Human Services Department, which may be called Department of Children and Family Services or Department of Jobs and Family Services.

For Veterans - There are programs available for Veterans. Check out the US Department of Veteran Affairs Vocational Rehabilitation and Employment Service page at http://www.vba.va.gov/bln/vre/. (This website was active as of initial publication of this book.)

For Entrepreneurs - The Small Business Administration. The website is: http://www.sba.gov/gcclassroom and as of this book's initial publication, training materials and online courses were available.

From Employment Agencies - Employment agencies may offer online training programs that are free to those who are registered with their agency. The training programs range from learning various computer software applications to obtaining certifications in concentrated areas - for example, in Human Resources for those who wish to take the PHR® (Professional in Human Resources) or SPHR® (Senior Professional in Human Resources) certification examinations.

Massive Open Online Course (MOOC) - Another area that is growing in popularity are MOOCs. MOOCs routinely enroll tens of thousands of students globally and the MOOCs often offer courses for free. Conduct an Internet search for available and affordable MOOC offerings.

OTHER THINGS TO KEEP IN MIND

Retirement Funds

DO NOT MAKE ANY WITHDRAWALS OF ANY KIND FROM ANY TYPE OF RETIREMENT ACCOUNT.

That 401K, IRA, public or federal employee retirement fund are all for just that purpose - RETIREMENT.

A Livelihood Transition is not planned retirement.

No matter what you think or how you try to forecast or rationalize, you will be hard pressed to make up any money that you withdraw from any retirement fund - no matter how young you are and no matter how much time you think you have to do so.

In addition to losing your retirement funds, there are TREMENDOUS tax penalties for making withdrawals from retirement accounts. Those tax penalties will eat up the money that you withdrew and leave it where the withdrawal amount received didn't give you any type of gain.

RETIREMENT ACCOUNTS ARE <u>NOT</u> SAVINGS ACCOUNTS FOR RAINY DAYS, EMERGENCIES, HEALTH CARE COSTS, HOME IMPROVEMENTS, OR MAJOR PURCHASES.

Retirement accounts are for RETIREMENT.

Retirement accounts are for RETIREMENT.

Retirement accounts are for RETIREMENT.

Retirement accounts are for RETIREMENT.

Any Type of Loan is a Guarantee to Your Financial Disaster

If you think you may have challenges, get some type of loan then watch your world truly crumble. There is nothing more delusional than an offer to receive money with no credit check. Receiving credit without a credit check is a loan with numerous astronomical fees and finance charges.

A loan is a loan and not a gift. A loan is money that is received but has to be paid back with an additional dollar amount. Getting a loan is not worth it to thwart eviction or repossession. Also, keep in mind that any type of advance is still a loan. It is borrowing against future money. At this stage in the game, you have to be sure you are counting chickens that have hatched and have a 99% chance they are going to survive and stay in your hand. During any period of an LT, the chickens that you do have in your hand are to put toward now and the future – not to take steps backwards and incur more debt in the long run.

Bankruptcy

Consult an attorney regarding this. Bankruptcy may be a great option AFTER you get yourself back on track with a stable source of income. During unemployment, new debts may arise that will not be covered in the bankruptcy. It would not make sense to file for bankruptcy before returning to a sense of stability.

Preventing Foreclosure

The Bank/Mortgage Company – As noted before, banks and mortgage companies are working with homeowners better than they were a few years ago.

Call your mortgage company or bank about your circumstances immediately. Keep in continuous contact with them regarding your situation and explore all programs that your mortgage company or bank offers.

Renting - Keep in mind that renting an apartment is typically less expensive than owning a home, especially with limited or no stable stream of income. You may want to explore the option of renting your home to carefully screened and qualified tenants while you move out into an apartment to rent. This option would be logical if:

- The rent amount is enough to cover the mortgage, insurance, and property taxes
- The tenant pays for all utilities and is responsible for landscaping/snow removal
- You have sufficient income to cover your own apartment rental costs

Short Sale – The option to sell your home for a dollar amount less than what you owe to the mortgage company to avoid foreclosure is a short sale. Consult a real estate agent that is experienced with these types of transactions and ask your mortgage company to share the details with you and your real estate agent regarding their process for short sales. This type of transaction is also called deed in lieu.

Mortgage Assistance Programs - BE LEERY of any mortgage assistance programs outside of the bank or servicing company who holds or services your mortgage. There are fraudulent schemes abound.

Avoid Falling Into Bad Check Systems

Having your name listed in a bad check system is a personal finance prison term of seven years unless you are able to pay off the outstanding balance. Being in this system keeps you from opening up free checking or savings accounts. The only checking or savings accounts that you will be able to open are second chance accounts that some banks are now offering which require a monthly fee to prove you're worthy to have a regular account with them.

Unfortunately, it does not matter if loss of income caused you to overdraw your account.

This is why it is very important to cancel all automatic debit payments and Internet banking payment schedules from your bank accounts.

Set Offer Acceptance Level Standards Early

Not only you want to have steady income, but the welfare system, the unemployment office, and the bill collectors want you to be employed. However, employment at any costs at any place for any price will not work in your favor. As noted before, do not accept an income opportunity that will not cover your expenses and get you back on track.

Only accept an opportunity or multiple opportunities that will yield income to allow you to return to the lifestyle in which you are accustomed with expenses covered including healthcare coverage, savings plans, and investments. You deserve the right to have that type of lifestyle.

Working for a Church

If you work for a church, you may not be entitled to unemployment because churches are not required to pay into unemployment. Before accepting an employment opportunity at a church or other non-profit organization, be sure to:

- Ask about the stability of the position and the organization given their current financial status and dependence on charitable contributions.
- Ask if the organization pays into unemployment.
- If they do not pay into unemployment, ask if the organization has a procedure in place to give ample notice and some sort of a helpful severance package should your employment ever be involuntarily terminated.

Working In An At-Will State

If you live in an at-will employment state, you can be terminated any time for any reason without any type of warning or severance package.

Unemployment and Personal Relationships

Lack of money can turn a sweet relationship sour. Lack of money can also cause someone to enter into a relationship or look for love in the wrong place for the wrong reason. Be continuously mindful that an LT can create conditions favorable for these types of relationship situations.

Receiving Advice From and Sharing Your Plans with Friend and Family

You may receive friendly and caring advice from friends and family regarding your employment situation. Immediately jump on any leads or reasonable suggestions that they may recommend.

As you brainstorm your destiny, be wary of sharing your dreams with everyone. Though your friends and family may have your best interests in mind and in heart, they may not understand your personal pursuits.

Guard your personal destiny from seeds of doubt and discouragement about your own dreams.

Your Time and Energy

It will take much focus and careful planning to balance income seeking efforts, bill collector communications, social service benefits management, and pursuing your dream. In a perfect world, it would be wonderful to divide your energy in four equal parts to address these activities.

Revisit from time to time to see what efforts are working and what results are you yielding from each activity.

There is a serious priority to keep food on the table, to keep the doctor at a phone call's reach and with open arms, and yet keep the roof over the head. It's a juggling act where you have to be focused and be creative.

This is why there is no room for self-pity, bitterness, or any other negative thinking.

Creating an Income Stream

I stumbled upon having multiple income streams by accident. When I was 20 years old, I worked at a retail department store while attending a business school for Secretarial Science. When I excelled in all the classes but was found twiddling my thumbs for a great part of the day, I was offered an opportunity to work a co-op for the afternoon at a major bank in the energy and human resources divisions. So I'd go to school in the morning, go to the bank in the afternoon, and then go to the retail department store in the evenings and on weekends.

Fortunately, when I was 22 and began joining great companies making more money, I was no longer eligible for the childcare voucher program, but my increased income was still not enough to cover the $400 to $500 a month in child care. I got a part time position in the evenings and on the weekends to pay for the day care so I could hold the full time position with the medical benefits.

Through my 20s and 30s, I held a full time position while either working a part-time job, becoming involved in a work at home opportunity, or all three. Though people thought (and commented I may add) that I was overly ambitious, greedy, crazy for working two gigs because "two gigs were for two people" yadda yadda yadda, that practice and industrious nature helped me during the seasons when there was no full time position with benefits - especially when I went through my personal LTs.

This personal account is shared to let the reader know that having multiple streams of income can keep things flowing when there is a blockage in one of the streams. There won't be need for panic, anxiety, fear, doubt, or worry.

If anyone has ever gone through an LT, the number one lesson that person has learned is that the employment opportunity they signed up for is not guaranteed and was never guaranteed.

It cannot be said enough. An employer is not the source.

One's livelihood, home life, and lifestyle stability cannot rest on the fact of holding a position at a company - even if the person is the business owner or an investor in the business.

A Controlling Factor

The greatest lesson of an LT is the realization of who is in control?

It would be ideal to create an income stream that is largely dependent on your vision, efforts, and results (and even better with the assistance of an organization of others that you have personally recruited - such as a business or multilevel marketing network).

Working for a company that identifies you solely by an employee number and the expense associated to the company's budget sheet does not offer the worker a strong base.

Strive for multiple streams of income. It's also important to strive to have an income that is not dependent on any type of eligibility criteria or funded by any type of service or program.

Do the Hustle

An unexpected LT is the crash course on the reality that one cannot count on having employment. An LT is the time to have a hustle mentality. It's time to seek out and develop multiple streams of income possibilities and to establish them quickly as was covered in the "Brainstorming Your Destiny" chapter.

How to Start

Don't know where to start? Type "How to Make Multiple Streams of Income" in your search engine on the Internet and about 1,290,000+ results will pop up in about 16 seconds.

WHEN INCOME BEGINS TO FLOW AGAIN

Continue to Live Well Below Means

Categorizing your expenses in the beginning was not just only an emergency first step exercise, but also to prepare and equip you with the tools and best practices to establish a lifestyle that if there is ever another LT, all expenses would be in order.

Continue Basic Lifestyle with Only "Got to Pay" Expenses and "Try to Pay" Expenses

Although income is flowing in again, continue to operate inside the budgetary system that you had during the LT period. For example, during the LT, Mary received $1,800 from benefits and other sources. Mary's new income opportunity is bringing in a steady $4,000 a month. Mary is still following the payment schedule for her expenses as if she were still only receiving $1,800 a month. Mary didn't restore her DSL or cable account nor did Mary go out and start spending and purchasing things even if those items were needed. Mary is not in a hurry to begin spending the extra $2,200 as yet because she has not yet established a solid wealth-building plan to do so.

Continue to be a good steward over your finances and continue to practice sound financial decision-making and spending habits. This new basic lifestyle of living will create great opportunities as you encounter additional increases in income.

The general rule is that when income increases your expenses should decrease. The extra money is seed money for college education funds; investments that are financial, business, or real estate-related; family trusts; — and yes, since life is for the living - extensive vacations, a new vehicle, a new home, etc.

Pay OFF the "Just Can't Pay Right Now" Expenses Immediately

First pay off the expenses that were in the "Just Can't Pay Right Now" category before implementing any of the ideas that were just previously mentioned. This is the time to pay off debt, return necessary accounts to good standing, and to fix or improve your credit rating.

TOOLS

Employment Application Log

The Employment Application Log is helpful to track employment applications made especially when following any unemployment compensation policies that require the reporting and recording of employment seeking activity.

The Type of Communication column can include:
- Phone Call
- Interview
- Application Made - Whether Online, Via Phone, or In Person

The Outcome column could include:
- Offer
- Not Hired
- 2nd Interview Scheduled
- Response with Next Steps
- Pending
- Specific details and log of all activity.

Additional Columns: Instead of having a growing or cluttered Outcome column, you may wish to add columns to cover various events such as: first interview, second interview, group interview, etc.

Creating an electronic spreadsheet to log employment application activity would assist in quickly editing and reformatting for additional information. Having to log on to use an electronic spreadsheet may seem cumbersome and extra work, but having an electronic spreadsheet offers the advantage of creating back-ups of the information along with the ease of neatly adding entries about application activity as you go along.

It may be a good idea to keep the user id and password information on this log in additional to another log where this information is recorded. For employment applications, do not use a user id or password that you use for your personal accounts such as banking, social media, etc.

Be sure to keep all e-mail messages confirming that your online application has been received. This will offer back up to your employment application declarations as well as assist you in remembering some of the details of when you made the application if you do not immediately record when you submitted an application.

For each position to which you apply, either printout or save as a PDF the job description. This will help you track what position(s) to which you applied especially if you have applied to many positions in one company. The saved PDF will also serve as a reference regarding the position to prepare for an interview, to develop talking points to highlight your experience, and to develop in-depth questions about the position.

EMPLOYMENT APPLICATION LOG								
Date	Contact Name	Company	Position of Interest	Address, City, State, Zip - Dept. Info If Any	Phone	Website	Type of Communication	Outcome

The Lender, Creditor, and Collections Log

This is a useful tool to track communications regarding payment arrangements or aggressive collection activities. It is better to have a log per company for easy access and reference.

Use the Detail section to capture full details of what was communicated, received, and/or sent between you and the company.

It would not hurt for this log to be placed in a designated folder along with any written communications between you and the company.

LENDER, CREDITOR, AND COLLECTIONS LOG							
COMPANY NAME					COMPANY PHONE NUMBER		
FULL ADDRESS							
ACCOUNT NUMBER		TYPE OF ACCOUNT/PURPOSE		WEBSITE		FAX NUMBER	
Date	TYPE OF COMMUNICATION	COMPANY REPRESENTATIVE NAME	REPRESENTATIVE PHONE NUMBER AND EXTENSION	DETAIL			

Bill Collector Letter Template

Your Street Address
Your City, State Zip
Current Date (Month Day, Year)

Bill Collector Company Name
Street Address
City, State Zip
Attn: Name or Department (if applicable)

Re: Acct: #_____
        Balance: $_____
        Monthly Payment: $_____

To Whom It May Concern:

Acknowledge the account and what your records indicate what is owed.

State what happened and include the date that the change took place.

State historical track record of making payments and to make a good faith statement that as soon as steady income resumes payment will be made or convey the payment amount that can be sent at the present time if applicable (but solely optional).

Sincerely,

(signature)

Your Full Name

Suggestion: If possible, obtain a PO Box as your permanent mailing address for all communications to come to the PO Box address versus to your home. Again, debt collectors use all information for the purpose of collecting a debt. Having a PO Box is good for all business-related communications. Select the PO Box with services that you desire at a rate in which you are most comfortable and able to pay as well as at a location where it is most convenient to commute from your home.

Sample of Initial Letter to Bill Collector

PO Box 893094Z
Moneytown, OH 44400*
September 23, 2013

Rung My Phone About Bills Company
321 Collections Street
Consistent, OH 44500
Attn: Collection Department

Re: Acct: #32090902BDL
       Balance: $5,309.00
       Monthly Payment: $169.00

To Whom It May Concern:

I am aware that I have an outstanding balance on the above-mentioned account.

The position I held was eliminated on September 15, 2013 and I am currently in a livelihood transition with no earned income.

As your records will show, I have been making regularly scheduled payments. I will resume making payments once I return to a steady stream of income.

Sincerely,

(signature)

Mia Ismy-Nameo

*Suggestion: If possible, obtain a PO Box as your permanent mailing address for all communications to come to the PO Box address versus to your home. Again, debt collectors use all information for the purpose of collecting a debt. Having a PO Box is good for all business-related communications. Select the PO Box with services that you desire at a rate in which you are most comfortable and able to pay as well as at a location where it is most convenient to commute from your home.

Payment Log

If you haven't already established this practice, keep a definite log of payments for the following:

- Rent/Mortgage
- Car Note
- Student Loan
- Back Tax Bills
- Any Other Creditor Account

By keeping this record, you will have documented proof of payment if any questions, court action, or discrepancy ever should arise.

Pay for these types of expenses either online or via money order. Although it is convenient and less expensive to pay by check, paying by money order or online is to obtain a receipt number from the money order or confirmation number that is generated online after the payment is received.

It would also be useful to capture where the money order was purchased. Money orders can be obtained from your banking institution, the United States Postal Service, as well as from some local convenience stores, gas stations (that offer check cashing or money order services), and most check cashing centers.

Although there is a record of payment if you pay by check from your checking account, your bank may charge you a fee per cancelled check to obtain a copy of cancelled checks should you need to produce evidence of payment history.

Internet banking places the control of sending the payment to the company out of your hands into the hands of your banking institution unless both your banking institution is able to send the payment and the creditor is able to receive the payment electronically - provided documentation of successful transmission.

The payment log on the following page is a sample of what to capture in payments for these very important accounts. This particular example is for a monthly mortgage payment. This person may want to consider paying their mortgage online so that the payment is received on or before the due date.

Creditor: Family Mortgage and Lending Enterprises

Date Purchased	Due Date	Payment	Money Order # /Confirmation Number	Institution	Payment Received on Time?
12/20/12	01/01/13	$890.00	3433220	My Regular Bank	Yes
01/19/13	02/01/13	$890.00	3987892	My Regular Bank	Yes
02/25/13	03/01/13	$890.00	3980984	My Regular Bank	03/02/13
03/21/13	04/01/13	$890.00	3909820	My Regular Bank	Yes
04/19/13	05/01/13	$890.00	39080984	My Regular Bank	Yes
05/15/13	06/01/13	$890.00	980322	My Regular Bank	Yes
06/25/13	07/01/13	$890.00	9380981	My Regular Bank	Yes
07/23/13	08/01/13	$890.00	39408085	My Regular Bank	Yes
08/18/13	09/01/13	$890.00	239801	My Regular Bank	Yes
09/21/13	10/01/13	$890.00	398430982	Credit Union	Yes

The log on the following page is an example if paying toward an arrearage along with the current payment. This person is following a weekly payment plan as agreed upon with the landlord once they began receiving income again. Around the week of May 24, the parties agreed to reduce the weekly amount. This person also keeps a running balance on how much they yet still owe and what they have paid thus far.

Services Communication Log

You may wish to keep a communications log as you establish various benefits, programs, and services while in an LT. Keeping a communication log per agency or organization can help you stay on track on what you need to do and provide as well as a reference to all communications made between you and the agency or organization.

Agency/Organization:						
Date	Time	Visit/Call	With Whom	Contact Info	Outcome	Next Step

Acknowledgements

First giving honor to God for blessing me
with the adventure of life.
Through the ups and shaken moments,
I have been given grand opportunity to learn so much.
It all has been for the unfolding Good.

~

To my circle of supportive family and friends.

~

To my children ~ the main reason why I continue to persevere.

ABOUT THE AUTHOR

Nicol has practiced in the areas of real estate, financial services, credit repair, and retail with over two decades in corporate training and development. Nicol is working on her first novel and second and third non-fiction works envisioned for 2014 publication.

Nicol enjoys spending time with her family, traveling, and creating empowerment avenues as well as philanthropic initiatives for women and children. Nicol is also an accomplished musician, actor, voiceover artist, and vocalist.

Nicol can be contacted at nicol@ladyintelligence.com and can be found on Facebook at www.facebook.com/nicol.indeed and followed at Twitter: www.twitter.com/nicol_indeed.

www.ladyintelligence.com

www.ingramcontent.com/pod-product-compliance
Lightning Source LLC
Chambersburg PA
CBHW050425290526
45786CB00003B/1401